Best Wishes

Frank Pearce

2002.

TORBAY
THE GOLDEN YEARS

TORQUAY, BRIXHAM & PAIGNTON IN THE 1950s AND 1960s

FRANK PEARCE

WITH PHOTOGRAPHS FROM THE TORQUAY MUSEUM COLLECTION

HALSGROVE

First published in Great Britain in 2002

British Library Cataloguing-in-Publication Data
A CIP record for this title is available from the British Library

ISBN 1 84114 208 5

HALSGROVE

Halsgrove House
Lower Moor Way
Tiverton, Devon EX16 6SS
Tel: 01884 243242
Fax: 01884 243325
email: sales@halsgrove.com
website: www.halsgrove.com

Printed and bound in Great Britain by Bookcraft (Bath) Ltd, Midsomer Norton

Contents

Acknowledgements   5

Foreword   7

Introduction   9

1   Glimpses of the Past   11

2   Enter the Golden Age   17

3   Fun in the Early Fifties   21

4   The Mid 1950s: Regattas and Royals   27

5   Mayflower Years: the Late 1950s   35

6   Out with the Old: 1959   47

7   Marching into the Sixties   59

8   Gateway to a New Era   83

9   'History is Now'   119

10   Torquay Museum   125

DEDICATION

To my wife Joan
for her constant support
and her many recollections.

Acknowledgements

The success in the compilation of this book has been due in no small way to the many kind friends and associates who have contributed photographs, documents and an assortment of memorabilia. Among those to whom thanks are due in particular are John Mann, Isabelle Barker, Marjorie Reeves, Ken Browse, Marion Gregory, Michael Collins, Linda Lewis, Stan Gregory, Derek Pearce, Max Danby, Chris and Linda Roach, Mike Sample, John Holmes and Alan Taverner.

As the major proportion of photographs came from the Torquay Museum I wish to record my sincere thanks to them, not only for this, but for the unstinting support and co-operation given by all the staff, particularly to Barry Chandler, librarians Michael and Lorna, and to Bob Philips.

THOSE OTHER DAYS

Though much is taken, much abides,
And though we are not now that strength which yet in other days
Moved earth and heaven : that which we are, we are,
One equal temper of heroic hearts,
Made weak by time and fate, yet strong in will,
To strive, to seek, to find, and not to yield.

Alfred Lord Tennyson

An aerial photograph taken over Torquay in 1947 showing the residential development on the high ground above Meadfoot. The curved terrace in the foreground is Hesketh Crescent, part of which includes the Osborne Hotel.

Foreword

Torbay - The Golden Years is an album of pictorial and literary recollections of life in Torbay's three towns Torquay, Paignton and Brixham, covering a decade or more during the 1950s and 1960s. The books aims to portray a period of hesitant evolution in which, like actors upon a stage we all played a part, however unimportant, however inconsequential. And although in this unfolding drama, with its transient highlights of joys and sorrows, of triumphs and disasters, the principal characters seemed indispensable, their retirement and absence from the glare of the spotlight caused no lasting impact on the saga we call life, for this play has no final curtain. Of equal importance, the book with its wealth of colourful local history reflects the cumulative efforts of those in authority who sought to build upon the steadily improving status of the Borough despite the adversities of modern trends. I invite you to look back and relive with me these golden years.

Frank Pearce
Paignton
August 2002

Introduction

When the dawn of the 1950s decade shed its early light on the United Kingdom, it revealed a thankful but exhausted country with many of its towns and cities pitted with craters and bombsites.

After five years of the horrors of the Second World War and after the fervour and euphoria of victory had faded, the country awoke to the realisation that it faced an era of change. And as memory pushes back the boundaries of history over fifty years we can see how the 1950s proved to be a Golden Age. Public figures were instinctively respected, parental authority and state law deferred to and although children often dissented, they grew up with some assurance of security and safety.

Following so closely after food and clothes rationing imposed by the Second World War, the British were certainly better off as unemployment declined and a measure of prosperity swept away the last traces of austerity. But even by 1950, the bacon ration was only three ounces a week. Ironically, the defeated enemy Germany, had by this time abolished food rationing altogether! However, in this country, there was a growing mood of cautious optimism.

While the decade may have had its setbacks, these were more than compensated by many stirring events, outstanding achievements in science, sport and the arts.

There was the beginning of a youth rebellion, a new sexual independence, but for the elderly, alarm as what they saw as a demolition of sexual morality. But when at the end of the decade the Conservative Prime Minister, Harold MacMillan, declared 'Most of our people have never had it so good', it seemed that most people had to agree with him.

This old water-trough once stood at the junction of Winner Street and Colley End. On hot summer days, thirsty cattle en route to the slaughter-house behind Crown and Anchor Way, would sometimes stampede down the hill to reach the water-filled fountain. On this site and prior to the fountain days, there stood a barn from which the old name Barn Hill originates. The archway just glimpsed on the right is part of the first Roman Catholic church built in Paignton. The thatched cottages in the background were demolished around the 1920s and the trough removed in February 1936.

1 – Glimpses of the Past

People are often accused of looking back to earlier times as to a Golden Age. The truth is that while life may have been less complex and communities more reliant upon each other's help, the decades running up to the 1950s were full of poverty and fear for many. Housing in Torbay's meaner areas was condemned as unfit for human habitation in the 1930s, but much remained a decade later along with the sickness and disease that went hand-in-hand with poor housing. Of course, the wealthier inhabitants and the holidaymakers enjoyed the undoubted delights the resort had to offer, even up to the brink of the Second World War. It was to be some years following that conflict that the country was able to return to normality but for many the world would never be the same again. Indeed the period 1939-1945 was a major watershed for twentieth-century society.

Here some of the residents of Conway Road, Paignton, celebrate VE Day in a well supported street party in the summer of 1945. In the foreground is Councillor George Stabb, Chairman of Paignton Urban District Council. Despite the public relief at the ending of the war in Europe the families of many servicemen still awaited news from the Far East. When Victory over Japan came there were renewed celebrations throughout the country.

Hundreds of thousands of American troops were based in South Devon including a large number in and around Paignton, prior to the invasion of Normandy on 6 June 1944. This 'Ticket Home' gun-crew contingent is the last to leave Paignton in 1947. They are left to right: Jonathon Adams, Johnstown, Pennsylvania; Carl Adorne, Akron, Ohio; Howard Canterbury, Bozoo, West Virginia; Charles Koral, Brooklyn, New York; Joseph Loughlin, Wilmington, Delaware; Lewis Pittenger, Newton, New Jersey; Sam Zora, Brooklyn, New York; Front row: Omar Choates, Little Crab, Tennessee; Lawrence Marion, Brooklyn, New York; Kenneth Boamley, Altona, Pennsylvania; Dominick Tufanio, New York; Wesley Antone, Tuscon, Arizona; Thomas Maffey, Ebenezer, Missouri; Vincent Ambrose, Bloomfield, North Dakota.

This historic photograph of Paignton's medical team (submitted by retired dentist Mr Michael Garry) shows the group outside Paignton hospital in 1948 on the day the National Health Service was launched. Back row left to right: Dr Paul Garry; Dr F. Grenier; Dr B.E. Tenison Mosse; Dr T. Sutton Coulson; Dr C. Lord Flood; Dr W.S. Empey; Dr R.S. Campbell; Mr A.D. Wall (surgeon); Captain Rosser (hospital secretary) Dr W.A. Reynolds. Middle row: Dr J.W. Bradbury; Dr H. Bumstead; Dr H.C. Adams, Miss Tickner (matron); Mr F. Green (hospital committee chairman); Dr A.T. Kennie; Dr C.H. Burridge. Front sitting: Dr J.Reeks, and Dr J.F. Burdon.

Above: *Dressed in their smart sailor suits, boys of the British Seamen's Orphan Boy's Home, Brixham, march to Sunday parade in 1936.*

Right: *The 57th Unit of the Brixham Sea Cadets in 1948.*

Below: *Prior to a march through the town in the 1960s, the band of the Orphan Boy's Home on parade.*

Left and below: *Chief Guide, Lady Baden-Powell reviews a march-past of Brixham Sea Rangers at Paignton's Oldway Mansion in 1949.*

In August 1954, Devon hosted its first Scout Jamboree for eighteen years at Watcombe, Torquay. It was an international event involving 2400 scouts from 13 countries occupying 120 sub-camp sites. The Jamboree was opened by the then Minister of Agriculture the Hon. Derek Heathcoat-Amory and was visited by Chief Scout Lord Rowallan. He is seen shaking hands with 15-year-old Alan Cornish, a member of the 5th Ellacombe Sea Scout's troop and holder of the Scout's V.C. Alan was awarded this for his courage and indomitable spirit after lying face-down on a wheel-chair, encased in plaster from head to foot, for five years.

Brixham Sea Rangers (above) *as a uniformed group prior to taking part in the Brixham Carnival of 1949* (below). *Among those in the group are Ruby Dickenson; Sylvia Doble; Isabelle Smardon; the Blackmore twins; Joan Harris; Pat Harley; Margaret Dyer; Molly Bourgoine; Celia Morris; Pat Gatehouse; Ann Brice; Nora Lambswood; Jennifer Simons and Valerie Clay. Also among the group is Miss Anne Hopkins who had the distinction of teaching Princess Elizabeth (the Queen) and Princess Margaret sea ranging skills in their teens. Skipper of the Sea Rangers, which was formed in 1941, was Miss Elizabeth Armitage. Following the christening of their vessel* SRS Churchill, *the Sea Rangers were known as 'The Winnies'.*

In 1861 William Gibbs took a house in Brixham for the care of the sons of deceased seamen. Over the years the home has been supported by voluntary contributions but in 1937 it was agreed that the home should be discontinued as a school with the boys in future attending the National School or the possibility of the Torquay Grammar School. The Brixham Sea Cadet movement was established in 1943.

Occasionally the home is visited by leading figures in the Royal Navy and sometimes members of the Royal family. This photograph is of the Countess Mountbatten's visit in September 1957.

2 – Enter the Golden Age

In 1951, a five-month celebratory occasion marked the end of post-war rationing and the centenary of the 1851 Great Exhibition opened by Queen Victoria in Hyde Park. At the centre of the 1951 Festival of Britain was an exhibition displaying British achievements in science and the arts, covering 25 acres of derelict land on London's South Bank. Here were erected the Dome of Discovery, the world's largest dome at the time, the 300 feet high Skylon Obelisk and the Royal Festival Hall. Further up-river at the Festival Pleasure Gardens in Battersea there were grottos and Mississippi showboat rides. The Festival was a great success attracting nearly ten million visitors. Regional attractions carried the celebrations to many millions more around Britain. The opening of the Festival was performed by King George VI in May 1951 with vast crowds determined to enjoy this special occasion.

The Festival of Britain site in London was dominated by the huge structure of the Skylon, a symbol said to represent the future soaring aspiration of the British people in 1951. Inset: The Festival of Britain logo. This, and the designs associated with the Festival influenced a generation of designers of everything from tableware to fashion.

The Coronation of Elizabeth II, on 2 June 1953, was an impressive State occasion demonstrating Britain's capability of staging awe-inspiring pageantry of regal grandeur. Despite the rain, an impressive procession of carriages with military and naval contingents paraded past pavilions and along streets lined with cheering crowds. To celebrate this special occasion many parties were held on Coronation Day throughout the Torbay area. This photo shows a children's party at Compton Place, St Marychurch visited by the Mayoral Party.

To mark the occasion of the Coronation of Queen Elizabeth II a street party was held in June 1953, in Palace Place, Paignton, for over 80 people, some of whom are wearing distinctive period costumes and hats. On the right is the Parish Church vicar the Reverend G.Pedley and Mrs Pedley.

Another Coronation street party, June 1953. War-time food rationing was barely over, yet the residents of Well Street, Paignton, found enough to organise this children's celebration party.

Coronation Walk, Babbacombe on the 19 November 1952. The ground lying to the north and west of All Saints Church, Babbacombe, was leased to the Corporation for 21 years by the Church Council at a low fee. It was laid out as an extension to Cary Park and the sapling that the Mayor of Torquay (Ald. T. J. Reeves Taylor) is here seen holding is one of the avenue of nearly forty flowering trees planted. Mr Ross Young, Parks Superintendent, is helping the mayor.

Opening Sherwell Valley housing estate in January 1953. The Mayor of Torquay unveils the tablet commemorating the opening. On the extreme right is the well-remembered Mr Rooke, secretary to many successive Torquay mayors.

In Devon, cities like Plymouth and Exeter were still trying to clear up after the bombing of the Second World War. Torquay's St Marychurch is seen here (above left) as the rubble is cleared away following the destruction of the Parish Church on 30 May 1943. On 27 March 1952 Aldermen and Councillors of Torquay attended a ceremony (above) on the site which marked the start of its rebuilding. Following its completion (left), the church was re-consecrated on 9 March 1956.

This was Watcombe Infant and Junior School's Opening Day in 1951. Many such new schools were built to accommodate the growing numbers of children from modern housing developments. This school served the rapidly growing housing estate at Watcombe.

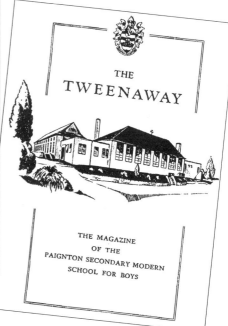

Some of the Masters and Boys of Tweenaway Secondary School in 1958.

In 1952, Paignton Secondary Modern School for Boys published its first magazine. This is the cover of the first edition.

3 – Fun in the Early Fifties

By mid-fifties, it was realised that not only had television come to stay, providing compulsive entertainment but that it was ruling the home, stifling conversation. Through the new media, new stars were being born overnight. In 1953 television's popularity helped bring about the demise of the Torquay Municipal Orchestra whose classical concerts gave so much pleasurable entertainment under the leadership of its popular conductor Ernest Goss to thousands of visitors and residents alike. It came as a bitter blow to the town. However local entertainment went on elsewhere. The cinema proved eternally popular, while the Brixham Operatic and Dramatic Society, born out of a concert party known as the 'Orange Bubbles', produced many shows among which were 'South Pacific', 'The Merry Widow' and 'The Wizard of Oz'.

Up to its closure Paignton Picture House had the singular distinction of being the oldest standing purpose-built cinema still in use in Western Europe. Its history reaches back to c.1909 and its final closure came on 25 September 1999. In the 1950s and 1960s it welcomed many stage and screen stars and notables of the period including Agatha Christie and the famous crime writer Edgar Wallace.

A staff party of the full complement of the Paignton Picture House in 1949.

The technical team of the Paignton Picture House, the Regent Cinema and the Adelphi Theatre, Derek Waddell, Arthur Tomlin and John Mann take a stroll between on-duty sessions in July 1955.

Many old Paigntonians will doubtless remember Mrs Olive Binmore, Manageress of the Picture House in the post-war years. Seen here (below) in 1955.

The magnificent building that housed Deller's Café will be remembered with affection, not only by Paigntonians, but by the residents of Torbay and the nearby towns and villages, and by thousands of holidaymakers. It was the fashionable venue for discerning customers throughout South Devon including cadets and their families from the Britannia Royal Naval College at Dartmouth. It was indeed an unhappy day for Paignton when this magnificent building fell to the savage claws of the bulldozers in 1965. (Inset) a detail from the superb art deco frontage of the Deller's building.

Prior to a Mr Lambshead building Deller's Café in Torbay Road in 1911, he owned a large frontage of shop premises in Palace Avenue known as Deller's Supply Stores, which in 1920 were bought by Chard Bros. They in turn sold out to Rossiters who now run it as Paignton's largest department store.

A group of the branch of the Paignton Women's British Legion at Deller's Café 1957. Seated front row is Councillor Tremeer.

Bridesmaids Patsy Webber and Sandra Binmore (below) *on the steps at Deller's Café c.1950.*

After attending to the needs of other revellers, the staff of Dellers took time off for their own party in 1953. Centre is the Manager Mr Craze and one time Chairman of the Paignton Urban District Council.

Peter Pelosi celebrating his 50th anniversary of trading in Paignton by distributing free ice creams to a crowd of eager children in 1953. He had kiosks in Torbay Road and Goodrington.

In 1954 Devon General Transport were proud to show off their new model bus, part of the new fleet of buses which was to ply between Paignton and Newton Abbot.

This photograph will be of interest to Paignton theatregoers of the 1950s. It is of Paignton Amateur Operatic Society's production of Iolanthe at the Palace Avenue theatre in 1955. The cast included Dora Deller, Ron and Mary Wellens, Joe Finch, Phyllis and Norman Elliot, Godfrey Farrant, Pat and Donald Wood, Molly Joiner, Gertrude Wyatt, Esmee Vowles, Dennis Isles, Bert Davey, Ernie Campion, Cliff Pritchard, Gloria Watkins, Ken and Doris Rowe, June Williams, Vera Whiting, and Charlie Patterson. Featured also was Bill Coysh as Chancellor, Pauline Norris as Phyllis, Jack Sanders as Private Willis, Marjorie Marriott as the Fairy Queen, and Alice Down as Iolanthe.

This photograph will doubtless evoke memories of long ago showing members of the Torquay Natural History Society's Annual Outing to Salcombe South Sands in June 1953.

On 20 September 1954, a plaque in Seaway Lane, was unveiled to the memory of William Froude who devoted much of his life and great intellectual powers to Admiralty experimental work. A Fellow of the Royal Society, he was a leading figure in the Devonshire Association. Seen here is Prof. H.F. Nordstrom of Gothenburg, some of Froude's descendants, the Mayor of Torquay, Councillor W. White, and Viscount Runciman who unveiled the plaque.

On the night of 4 July 1952, a serious fire broke out in the building known as Waycotts Corner, Paignton. By morning, Waycotts house agents and adjoining premises either side had been completely destroyed. These included such shops as Purdy's tobacconists, Brounette's gowns and Maynard's sweets. Following the rebuild the corner is now occupied by house agents Wilkins & Partners.

4 – The Mid 1950s: Regattas and Royals

By the mid-fifties the towns of Torbay were discovering the new-found confidence that was also to be felt in the rest of the country. The post-war boom in building, rising employment, and the status of Britain within the world as a whole, brought about a feeling that we were indeed entering a Golden Age. To the resorts all this meant full summer bookings and packed beaches under summer skies. While holidaymakers arrived by their thousands by train, and increasingly in cars, the local population continued to entertain themselves with their traditional summer events, including regattas, fetes and carnivals.

A sight to gladden any true yachtsman's heart. Yachts under full sail skim past the camera in one of Torquay Regatta's racing events in 1954.

Over the years, Torquay bowling club has made a considerable contribution to the sporting activities of the town. Sunshine welcomes the Ladies section of the Torquay Bowling Club (right) *on their opening day Easter Monday 1965. This event* (below) *is Captain's Day in August 1951 with the captain Jose Casanova* (standing sixth from left in glasses).

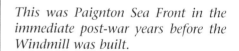

This was Paignton Sea Front in the immediate post-war years before the Windmill was built.

The same scene but after the attractive illuminated windmill was built in the early 1950s.

Having assembled at the Torquay Bus Station, the 1954 Torquay Carnival begins its parade along Lymington Road via Castle Circus to the Strand and Sea Front.

In the company of a sartorially elegant groom, the carnival queen and her maids of honour join the parade in the 1954 Torquay Carnival.

With acknowledgements to the late Leslie Pateman's Pictorial Survey of Babbacombe and St Marychurch, these are scenes he captured from their 1955–56 Annual Charity Carnival Fayres. Above: Secretary Leslie Pateman sorts out the prize distribution assisted by Councillor Bert Waddling and Chairman Leonard Newman.

Above: *The children's Box Car race 1956.*

Left: *Waitresses compete in a race from Chilcote Memorial to Babbacombe Downs 1955. Leader and eventual winner of the race was Mrs Joyce Metcalf.*

The popular comedian Arthur English assists at the Babbacombe Carnival, June 1956.

A group in the 1956 Paignton Carnival. They were dressed in Toreador costumes to represent the theme of the show at the Paignton Green tent theatre where the well-known tenor Lester Ferguson and the Charles Shadwell band were appearing.

The group photo is the Browse staff outside their Torbay Canning Factory in 1956. This photograph and those below will evoke many memories among those who recall Paignton Harbour in pre-war years.

This old photograph dates from the early 1920s. The motor launch White Rose *built by Louis Gale had been commissioned by a director of Tate & Lyle Sugar Co. The occasion was its christening by 12 year old Stella Gale on the slipway adjacent to the Gale yard.*

Louis Gale on the right and his colleague Harry Patterson.

On the same side of the harbour where stood Louis Gales's boat building yard, there now stands Browse Bros busy crab meat processing factory. In 1923 Maurice Browse ran four pleasure boats and five crab boats from Paignton harbour, he also had a successful seafood stall on Paignton front for 16 years, where now stands the new cinema. Far left: Maurice Browse (centre) with two of his staff. Left: Maurice's son, Ken Browse, who took over from his father. His two sons, Ben and Peter now run the business.

A section of Paignton's Women's British Legion in carnival team spirit, 1956.

A mass gathering of Rotarians and their wives at Paignton's Palace Hotel in 1952. The members were drawn from districts in Devon and Cornwall.

Three photographs taken during the visit of Her Majesty Queen Elizabeth II to Torquay on 8 May 1956. Above: HM The Queen at Torre Abbey. Right: the Queen, escorted by the Mayor of Torquay councillor K.R.Bryant, and the Duke of Edinburgh by the Lord Lieutenant of Devon, Earl Fortescue, are seen passing through the Mohun gatehouse at Torre Abbey. Below: The evening reception at the Torquay Town Hall. A glittering occasion attended by many well-known celebrities, notables and local worthies.

5 – Mayflower Years: the Late 1950s

Already the winds of change were sweeping over Torbay, with the old ways giving way to the new. The traditional industries of the region, including fishing, were moving out of the hands of individual fishing families who were replaced by large companies. New schools reflected the trend towards a meritocracy, where anyone could succeed through dint of education and hard work. The old social barriers were slowly being dismantled, just as the old familiar faces of the towns themselves were undergoing change. The car was the new force in transport, representing individual wealth, choice and a new sense of personal freedom.

Work in progress on the extension to Princess Gardens in 1959. This is a view from Princess Pier of the two-tier circular promenade which was opened by the Mayor Ald. J.F. Haarer on 29 July 1959. It is a section of the Torquay improvement scheme started in 1939 by Mr P.W. Ladmore and completed by his successor as Borough Engineer Mr F. T. Nixon.

A fountain plays in the centre of the completed Princess Gardens promenade c.1960.

Though the war had ended more than a decade earlier, memories of those who had been lost were fresh in the minds of the living. On the 2 June, 1957, a conference of men and women of RAF Associations held a meeting at Torquay Pavilion to discuss the welfare of the disabled airmen of the First and Second World Wars. Later, Lord Tedder, Marshall of the RAF, laid a wreath on the Torquay cenotaph in memory of those who had died.

One of the most important church services of the year and dear to the fishermen of Brixham is the annual Harvest Festival of the Sea held at All Saint's Church. Here in 1957 Burgees from local fishing smacks are being used as decoration.

Among the many new building projects underway in the late 1950s was the commencement of the building of Churston Grammar School in 1957. This photograph shows the installation of the electricity supply with foreman of works Alfred Mann, Ted Turnstool and Alec Hayman.

Torquay's new fire station based in the Newton Abbot road was officially opened on 8 October 1957, by Sir George Hayter-Hames, chairman of Devon County Council. Even as the ceremony was taking place, alarm bells activated two appliances which had to race away at full speed.

The Duchess of Kent and the Mayor, Councillor E.G. Milford, departing from Torre Abbey on the occasion of the Duchess opening the new Catering Department of the Torquay Technical College on 15 October 1958.

This new First-Aid Post (below) replaced the St John's Ambulance Brigade's tent on Abbey Sands. It was erected by the Torquay Corporation in Abbey park Gardens in 1958. On left of door is the Mayor (Alderman L. Goodrich) supported by Mr Knapman (Chairman Ambulance Association), Mrs Goodrich, Miss Collihole, Mrs Currie and Mrs Harvey. On the right of the door are Divisional Surgeon A.V. Currie and Supt. Diamond.

The visit of Countess Mountbatten to Paignton in 1957. At this time the Countess was Superintendent-Chief of St John's Ambulance. It was in this capacity, and as Chairman of St John and Red Cross Service Hospitals Welfare Dept, that she left for a ten week tour of Cyprus and the Far East in January 1960, but died in her sleep during the night of 20 February in North Borneo, aged 58.

A familiar sight at Cockington's famous Drum Inn in 1958. After partaking of the customary stirrup cup the meet await the Master of the Hounds signal for the 'off'. Reserve hip-flasks have already been carefully concealed.

Aided by the Corporation, Torquay's open-air theatre was a voluntary venture which lasted from 1950 to 1958. On fine evenings plays were enacted outside the old tithe barn with a deck chair audience. In inclement weather the barn interior was used.

In September 1958 national sheepdog trials were held at Petitor. Here, in the closing stages of this trial the watching sheep-dog awaits the final move.

The discovery of fossilised bones when the road under King Street, Brixham, was dug to lay water pipes in 1958, presented a mystery until their classification by the British Museum. They were at first thought to be a Bronze-Age burial but were later confirmed to be not earlier than around AD1680 to 1710. The several complete sets of male bones therefore suggest they were buried around the same time as the landing at Brixham of William, Prince of Orange, in 1688. In this group Mr Guy Belleville (in white coat) and Mr W. Saxton, Clerk to the Council, examine some of the remains.

In 1958, Excavations at Broadsands, Paignton revealed an ancient tomb in which interesting pieces of pottery were found by members of the D.A.E.S. Left to right are Mr C.A. Raleigh Radford, Chairman Paignton U.D.C., Mr Guy Belleville, Sir Cyril Fox, Lady Aileen Fox, Miss Gosney (back to camera) and Mrs Belleville.

A replica of the original Mayflower *which sailed from Plymouth, England in 1620 was built at Upham's shipyard, Brixham during the years 1955–56.*

Following the laying of the keel, expert craftsmen and artisans were employed to create an accurate copy of the original, able to withstand the violent storms of the Atlantic Ocean. The little ship under the command of Captain Alan Villiers arrived off the US coast to be greeted by an escort of British and American ships; the highlight being a salute by the Aircraft Carrier, Ark Royal. Mayflower II's *final destination was Plymouth, Massachusetts, where the Pilgrim Fathers first landed.*

Sails filled in a light breeze, racing yachts sail across the waters off Oddicombe beach in the 1958 Babbacombe Regatta.

Dr Basil Halliwell unveils the tablet to commemorate the opening of the new X-Ray Department at Torbay Hospital on 10 December 1958 and in memory of his father Dr John Halliwell.

St Marychurch Church of England Primary School was destroyed by enemy bombers in the Second World War. In November 1958, after a short service in the rebuilt church attended by a very large congregation and the Mayor and Mayoress of Torquay Mr and Mrs E.G. Milford, the new building was officially opened and blessed by church dignatories including Dr Mortimer, Bishop of Exeter, Canon E. F. Hall, Archdeacon of Totnes, and the Vicar, Rev T. P. Vokes-Dudgeon.

On 25 July 1958 Princess Alexandra of Kent performed the ceremony of naming Brixham's new lifeboat. The vessel cost £38 000 and purposed to serve the whole of Torbay. Standing in the stern is the Bishop of Plymouth who dedicated the vessel, with the Chairman of the Urban District Council, Mr Guy Belleville.

Sir G. Hayter-Hames C.B.E. unveils the tablet commemorating the opening of Fernicombe Service Reservoir in 1957, supported by the Chairmen of the two Urban District Councils of Paignton and Brixham. The reservoir, situated on heights above Brixham and Kingswear, serves both towns.

Here (below) in February 1957, the new electricity sub-station was opened at Tweenaway bringing a direct power line from Newton Abbot. Mr A.W. Allwood (district manager of SWEB is showing Cllr A. C. Jenkins around the new station).

Fifteen years after the end of the war in Europe, Torquinians gather at the Torquay seafront Cenotaph in 1959 to remember the dead of two World Wars 1914–18 and 1939–45. The last-post, the two minute silence, the silent vigil of four Royal Marines and the bowed heads of the spectators reflect the mood of this sombre occasion.

Torquay Cricket Festival 1958 - England versus the Commonwealth. The Visitors – left to right back row: J. Manning (Australia), K.Barrington (Surrey), K.Andrew (N.Hants), F.Titmus (Middx), I.Titmus (Middx), P Height (West Ind), T.Lock (Surrey), R.Willson (Torquay). Middle row: S Bullen (Umpire), Hamif Mohammed (Pakistan), A.Taylor (Essex), R.Illingsworth (Yorks), C.Smith (West Ind), Brian Close (Yorks), L.Fuller (S.Africa), C.McCool (Aust), - Price (Umpire). Front row: L.Jackson (Derby), Gary Sobers (West Ind), G.Gladwin (Derby), R.Simpson (Notts), D.Haines (Hon Sec), V.Jackson (Aust), D.Brookes (N.Hants), D.Kenyon (Worcs), F.Worrell (West Ind).

With a fair wind and full sails, the yacht Tomboy *speeds past Livermead during the Torquay regatta of 1958.*

Fashionably dressed summer visitors to Cockington in 1958 inspect the complimentary letters sent from all parts of the world and pinned up outside the old forge.

This attractive picture shows parts of Torquay Strand, Fleet Street and Vaughan Parade lit up at night during the Christmas period 1959. The illuminated Christmas tree is by the slipway to the Inner Harbour and the cross in the night sky, that on the tower of St John's church.

Snowfalls are indeed a rarity in Torbay's warm climate, yet here on the greensward opposite Torbay Hotel in the winter of 1958–59 a fair sprinkling of snow transformed the scene.

The Torquay Leander Swimming and Life Saving Society's Boxing Day Morning dip was one of Torquay's outstanding season's events. In this photograph of the 'dip' in 1958 hundreds of onlookers watch as a few intrepid bathers test Torbay's icy waters.

6 – Out with the Old: 1959

On the threshold of the 1960s it is worth remembering that the comparative dourness of the previous decade was very much the legacy of the Second World War. But whilst rationing lasted into the early years of the 1950s and unemployment for returning servicemen remained a problem for the government, the rising sense of optimism in Britain eventually swelled and burst into that psychedelic shower that became the 'swinging sixties'. In the older generation the sense that 'anything goes' fuelled a reaction against change, and against the young in particular, but this only further encouraged Rebellious Youth. The truth may be that the rebellion was largely one associated with fashion and music, and that the pattern of life for many went on pretty much as before. Even so many who might have known better were caught up in the feeling that all that was old was bad, and it was in this period that so many of the towns of Britain suffered a far worse fate at the hands of the planners than Hitler had ever achieved. In Torbay, however, there was a great deal of poor housing that quite properly became victim to the bulldozer.

These houses in Melville Street were built as early as 1850 and by the 1950s they had become so derelict that the Town Council made compulsory purchase orders for sixteen dwellings which were unfit for habitation. There are flowers in pots on the windowsill of No. 24 whose owner was the last to resist the purchase order.

Another view of Melville Street prior to the houses being cleared for a car park.

A tiny midget submarine manned by her crew of three slowly drifts into Torquay Harbour in 1959. These vessels did sterling work in the Second World War by entering enemy waters and sinking anchored shipping.

A fine view of Torquay's Outer Harbour as seen from Rock Walk in 1959.

Torquay in 1959, showing the quays and Inner Harbour.

A crowd gathers on the South Pier, Torquay Inner Harbour, on 15 April 1959. They are watching salvage operations on the motor launch Zephyrus which had sunk overnight. The fault appeared to arise from water entering through the exhaust ports.

This capsized barge off Daddyhole Plain is the result of a violent storm which hit Torbay on the night of 7 December 1959. She was one of three being towed by a Dutch tug and from which one of the two man crew was lost. Capsized, she was carried past Haldon Pier and ran ashore near Palm Court Hotel.

In August 1959, Ald. F. March, representing Torquay Town Council at Exeter airport, welcomed civic dignitaries. He is seen shaking hands with the Lord Mayor of Leeds. Behind her are the Lord Mayor and Lady Mayoress of Bradford. On the far right is the managing director of the airline and above him the chairman of Clyst Honiton RDC which controlled the airport.

Above: *the opening of the new X-ray department in Torbay Hospital September 1959. Col. H.A. Guy, Chairman of the S.W. Regional Hospital Board, is seen cutting the ribbon across the entrance.*

Above: d*eclaration of poll, General Election October 1959. On the balcony of the Town Hall are (l–r) Mr W.V. Cooper (Lab) partly hidden Mr F.M. Bennett (Con) and Mr T. Kellock (Liberal).*

Above: *the Lord Mayor of London Sir Harold Gillett gives his address at the annual meeting of the Association of Municipal corporations at the Torquay Pavilion in September 1959.*

The exhibition, held at Torre Abbey in October 1959, was to mark the 25th Anniversary of the founding of the Women's Voluntary Service. Seen (l–r) is Brigadier Spencer OBE, County Civil Defence Officer; Dowager Lady Hillingdon, Vice Chairman WVS; Mrs Croft Fors, Civil Defence Instructor (demonstrating radio activity instrument) and Mrs E. L. Haggard, MBE, centre organiser Torquay WVS.

In 1959 distinguished visitors attended the Centenary of the Brixham Boy's Home. On the left are Lord Churston, Committee Chairman and Admiral Sir Richard Onslow, Commander in Chief, Plymouth Command. On right is Lord Roborough, Lord Lieutenant of Devon.

Here in the precincts of the ruined St Marychurch parish church, Aldermen, Councillors and others attend the service to mark the start of rebuilding, 25 March 1952.

A magnificent photograph of the Band of H.M. Grenadier Guards marching along Torquay seafront on 7 August 1959, headed by the immaculately uniformed Drum Major, H.J. Tilley. The band were on a recruitment drive in the westcountry and, following the parade, a concert was held on the seafront.

The Patronal Festival at St John's Church, Torquay, May 1957. Three Bishops are present: the most Rev E.F. Paget, former Archbishop, Central Africa, Dr R.C. Mortimer of Exeter and Dr J.C. Ward of London.

A new organ was installed in St John's in 1959. When Canon Robinson founded the Choir School in 1871, he set a high musical standard for St John's. A notable organist was Henry Ditton Newman (1879–85) whose memory had been kept alive for over 70 years by the report that he still continues to haunt the Vicarage (once the Choir School) and the Church. It was hoped that the installation of the new organ would show that the 'ghost' music was really mechanical in origin. Other well known organists in the past have been Dr Harold Rhodes and Mr Vernon Read.

When water skiing came to Torquay in 1958 it set an appetite for the new water sport which quickly grew in popularity. Here is a double tow from a speed-boat across Torbay's calm waters.

A crowded Paignton beach, midsummer 1959, with all the best ingredients to make it into a carefree holiday. Brilliant sunshine, calm bathing water, deckchairs, ice creams, and an eagerly awaited Punch and Judy Show in the foreground.

A party enjoying an organised tour of Babbacombe Downs in 1959. The Downs, rising almost perpendicularly from the sea for 300 ft, command a magnificent prospect overlooking Babbacombe Bay, Oddicombe Beach and Babbacombe beach. From these white marble beaches, red sandstone cliffs rise abruptly to contrast vividly with the green above and the sea below. A spectacle of outstanding beauty of which returning visitors never tire.

A busy shopping morning as Torquay's Fleet Street creates a crowded scene in 1959, with two-way traffic and hundreds of pedestrians (some having to walk in the road). Such scenes brought early warning signs for town planners for whom the growing numbers of cars presented increasing problems.

These two pre-war photographs illustrate the changes that have since taken place around the harbour area. Before the days of demolition Torquay Harbour was home to a prosperous fish-market which served Torquay and the nearby precincts. Elderly Torquinians will remember this wide space was also occupied by large coal-stores and the Coast Lines Stores. Here also was the Harbour Master's office situated just at the entrance. This photograph dates from the late 1930s, before the D-Day slipways had been built.

An unusual view of Beacon Quay around the late 1930s with Beacon Hill on the left and the Marine Spa in the background. Behind the parked cars are (left to right), the Harbour Master's office, the Coast Lines stores, and beyond a row of large coal stores which were supplied by coal barges like those shown in the foreground. Much of the coal from these stores fed the large boiler house in the Marine Spa which supplied hot water for the medical section, the heated swimming bath and the great ball-room.

While the preceding photographs show Torquay Harbour in its industrial days, by the late 1950s many of its former buildings had been swept away. This photograph, taken in 1959, reveals the transition between working port and the harbour area being devoted to tourism and leisure boating.

In 1959 workmen tunnelling under Union Street near Castle Circus to install a new main drain found an old culvert. Records suggest it may have been part of a scheme devised in 1881 for carrying off storm water and thus preventing the flooding of Union Street and Fleet Street.

7 – Marching into the Sixties

Torbay entered the 1960s amid the noise and chaos of demolition and rebuilding work. With a new-found prosperity, holidaymakers demanded greater luxury and more diverse entertainment, while residents of Torbay looked for a reduction in the traffic congestion and easier parking which the old town layout would not accommodate. These factors were just part of the general movement towards a new town layout and anyone who remembers those years will certainly recall that the area, at times, resembled one huge building site.

Against this background the town started the decade with an eager sense of the future. Tourists continued to flock here in their hundreds of thousands. The advent of cheap package tours to foreign resorts had yet to make its mark.

This picture, taken in April 1962, shows the replica of Drake's ship the Golden Hind *at rest in calm water in Torquay Inner Harbour. It was built to appear in the Westward Television series on the life of Sir Francis. The twenty-unit troupe of the British Seamen's Orphan Boy's Home, Brixham, are drawn up on Haldon Pier to welcome its arrival. Colin Smith, aged 9, the drum major, on the left, heads the procession.*

Sir Richard Gould (Secretary of the NUT) plants a tree at the opening of the Sherwell Valley County Infants School in June 1960. Present were the county architect Mr R.N. Guy, the Vicar of Cockington, the Rev F. Roy Chatfield and the Rev J. Pickering.

A wonderful summer scene across the beautiful bowl that comprise the lawns surrounding Cockington Court. Amid the beautiful and venerable surroundings of Cockington Village, children of Torwood School dance round the Maypole on a fine sunny day in July 1961.

Torquay Leander Swimming Club's Boxing Day dip at Beacon Cove in 1961. Overlooking the cove is the old Marine Spa showing the magnificent Vita Glass sun lounge/coffee lounge which was frequented by thousands of visitors and residents alike.

An interesting contrast with the photograph above - a crowded Oddicombe beach on a fine summer's day in 1960 with the terminus of the cliff railway in the background. Several dinghys (sails set) await launching.

Torquay Strand in 1960. On the right in the foreground is Bobby's, the popular ladies and gentlemen's store for much of Torquay's dress conscious clientele. Upstairs it had a superb restaurant with unrestricted views overlooking the harbour and crowded yacht moorings. Bobby's restaurant became the fashionable meeting place for afternoon tea along with its regular musical accompanists.

Paignton Green in 1960 hosted a Veteran Car Rally. As can be seen the occasion was well supported with veteran cars from all parts of the British Isles.

A crowded Babbacombe Downs with its side-shows and numerous stalls, on the occasion of the 1960 Babbacombe Regatta. Below the headland, in the distance, can be seen a part of Oddicombe beach.

Chelsea Pensioners sign the visitor's book at Oldway Mansion Paignton in the presence of one of the last Chairmen of Paignton Urban District Council, Mr Frank Martin, before the area became the Torbay County Borough.

Autumn in Lymington Road.

St Luke's near Shedden Hill, Torquay, was another church which suffered from German bombers. Here, during rebuilding, the vicar Rev W.H. Ryder-Jones, stands on the top-most platform of the tall steeple for a re-dedication service.

An auspicious occasion with the opening of Torquay's new Court House by Lord Morris on 11 April 1960. In centre Lord Morris with the Mayor, Alderman J.F. Haarer and the Deputy Mayor Major H. Stanway, the Mayor's Chaplain (Canon Boers), Mr T. Adams the Town Clerk, Mr T. Williams and Mr W. Bourne.

One of the last pictures of Torquay fishermen mending their nets on the South Pier in 1960. In the years that followed, vast changes were to take place in the Beacon Hill area. The famous Marine Spa was demolished, Beacon Cove closed and all to make way for an entertainment complex that financially failed, leaving the area as a barren wasteland.

A reminder of past splendours: a night scene of the Marine Spa in her glory days c.1935.

Synchronised swimmers at the Marine Spa in the 1950s.

Under a storm of public protest, the dismantling of the Torquay Marine Spa in 1971 was an extreme example of the modern trend. Thousands of visitors to Torquay were drawn to the famous Marine Spa with its magnificent ballroom, where excellent orchestral music could be enjoyed during the day and where some of the best dance bands in the country played at night. Also in this superb building, modern medical baths were complemented by elegant lounges and a wonderful vita-glass sun-lounge restaurant with incomparable views of the whole of Torbay. The building also housed an indoor, heated salt-water swimming bath and it was here during the early 1950s that the Torquay Leander Swimming club introduced its famous Water Ballets of synchronised swimming to music by teams of champion girl swimmers. Most times these were presented to capacity houses and became part of Torquay entertainment.

This picture of the Old Mill in Littlegate Road, Paignton, confirms that it was a building of considerable size. The overflow of water which Bishop's Palace took from Waterleat along the leat in Winner Street flowed into this area of Littlegate Road and became known as The Mill Pool. The Mill was demolished in the 1960s.

On 23 December 1960, Plainmoor Football ground had its first experience of the new floodlighting. The lights were projected from four 80ft high pylons carrying sixteen high-powered lamps. At a Valuation Court on 30 May 1961, however, residents registered complaints of noise and glare and as a consequence rating reductions were made.

In June 1960, the Duke of Edinburgh arrived at Torre Abbey meadows in a scarlet coloured helicopter piloted by himself. The occasion was to address the conference of the British Medical Association. Later he left Wall's Hill for Exeter.

While the spires of Oxford's colleges may contemplate its seats of learning, three of Torquay's church spires consider the panorama of Torquay's golden bay. From left to right: St Lukes, St Mary Magdelene, Upton; and Belgrave Congregational Church, seen here in 1960.

Right: *two smartly uniformed and bemedalled Chelsea pensioners receive a warm welcome on a visit to Oldway in 1960.*

Below: *presentations at the Town Hall on 5 April 1961 conferred the Freedom of the Borough on three former Torquay Mayors and County Councillors. On left is Cllr. F. J. March, senior member of Council. Centre is Col Rowland Ward and right Cllr C.T. Bowden.*

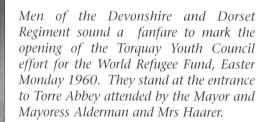

Men of the Devonshire and Dorset Regiment sound a fanfare to mark the opening of the Torquay Youth Council effort for the World Refugee Fund, Easter Monday 1960. They stand at the entrance to Torre Abbey attended by the Mayor and Mayoress Alderman and Mrs Haarer.

Whitbread's Yard in Church Street, Paignton, at one time Starkey, Knight and Ford, and now the site of St Johns Court Flats which extend down into Princes Street and Littlegate Road. This is a sensitive conservation area of Paignton.

Torquay Road, Paignton, in its two-way traffic days c.1960, looking north towards Hyde Road Corner, Gerston Hall on left. On right is Stephens' Ironmongery, Frank Martin's furniture store and Newstead House owned at this time by Bain (dental surgeon). Demolished to make way for the new Post Office.

Tor Hill, Torquay, 1962. On the right is the Zion Methodist Church built in 1863 and at its side, a new venture the Marsham Tyre Co Ltd which replaced a large wholesale fruit and potato store.

Grange Cottage Goodrington. In 1960 these two old cottages stood in the lane behind Waterside. The photograph was taken in April of that year just before the area was used as a large caravan site.

An eventual victim of the clearances in Winner Street, this is Torbay Mills premises in Paignton. The company also had a number of other shops in South Devon but this one did not survive the demolition of this area in the 1960s.

This building and shop once stood at the top end of Church Street, Paignton, at its junction with Winner Street. At one time the building had shops on three sides, all of which succumbed to the bulldozers in the early 1960s.

The Croft Hotel was a well-known land-mark in the town and a popular place for holiday-makers. It was demolished in the early 1960s to make way for the busy Crossways shopping centre.

The clearance of the site on which the Croft Hotel and other buildings once stood (in the early 1960s) ready for development into what is now Crossways Shopping Centre, Paignton.

The superb photograph catches the elegance of a visiting Spanish Sail Training ship at anchor in Torbay in 1960. She is officially described as a Barquentine.

Brixham Western Lady *motor launches provide a constant ferry service between Brixham and Torquay and have done so for over fifty years. The trip across Torbay takes 25 minutes and is considered by many as a preferable alternative to other modes of transport in Torquay. The* Western Lady *craft are all ex-Royal Naval Coastal Forces Fairmile Motor launches. In high season it is a fascinating sight to see the* Western Lady *lit overall with fairy lights on a summer evening taking passengers to view the full splendour of Torbay.*

A swarm of gluttonous seagulls descend on the Silver Star II fishing boat secured at Beacon Quay with a fresh catch of mackerel. Though greatly in decline, fishing boats such as this still ply their trade from the harbours of Torbay.

Construction of the new Beacon Quay car park in early 1961.

This photograph of Waterside Holiday Camp in Dartmouth Road, Paignton, was taken in 1955, just as cars and camping were beginning to emerge as a cheaper form of holiday, after the austerity of five years of war. It is included here in contrast to the picture below. The only provisions were a tent, a small camp shop and some toilets and perhaps a small caravan if you were well off. Waterside was owned by a group of local businessmen until the mid 1930s when it was sold to the Paignton U.D.C. for £17 000. Prior to the purchase by the Council, a Mr and Mrs Corney managed the camp living in the detached house nearby. Main drainage did not arrive at the camp until 1953.

The ever popular Goodrington pleasure park, Youngs Park, as it was in 1964. In the few years between these two photographs being taken, the level of entertainment and comfort demanded by holidaymakers had seen a signifcant increase. In the foreground is the model-boat lake and beyond, the pleasure boating lake.

The tiered car park off Beacon Hill was opened on 23 June 1961. Within an hour, its top tier was already full.

A 1960 photograph of the home of celebrated scientist and mathematician Oliver Heaviside in Warberry Road. He came to live here in about 1910 when the house was called Homefield. A Fellow of the Royal Society he never married and died in a Torquay nursing home in 1925. The building later became the Killester Hotel.

In February 1961 the Torbay Yacht Club decided to amalgamate with its neighbour, the Corinthian Yacht Club so that the combined club could retain Royal status. The original RTYC was founded in 1863 and members came from all parts of Britain in their large yachts, then in fashion, to take part in the local regattas. Here shown are its premises on Beacon Hill. During World War II, the premises were taken over the by RAF.

Chairman of Paignton Urban District Council (Mr G. Walke) unveils a plaque to mark the opening of a new block of flats for elderly people. The flats, are named after Mr J. Kingsland, Chairman of the Housing Committee, who is standing next to Mr Walke.

One of the new factories opened in Torbay in the early 1960s. These premises in Woodland Road, were built for the Sifam Electrical Instrument Co Ltd, and were opened on 9 December 1960 by Mr F.M. Bennett, MP for the Torquay Division.

Above: *this picture was captured in 1960 in Queen Street, Torquay after mothers petitioned the Council for a playground alleging the street was too dangerous. The children's excellent condition contrasts sharply with their homes some of which were due for demolition.*

Trampolines erected at Goodrington during the 1960s proved very popular. Youngsters were demanding much more sophisticated entertainment in this decade, a great difference to the simple toys of earlier times. Later all this area was taken over by the Quay West development.

The demolition of the old Woolworth building in Station Square, Paignton, in 1963, prior to rebuilding.

Traffic from both directions stops in Torbay Road, Paignton, at the rail crossing while the London bound train goes through. The photograph was taken c.1969. On extreme left is the new Woolworth's store.

8 – Gateway to a New Era

While much of the traditional way of life continued in Torbay, major changes to the fabric of the towns and to its social structure were well underway by the mid 1960s. Whilst the advent of new technology spelt the end of many crafts and skills, it also brought new jobs to the region and affected everyone's lives. On the back of this grew the need for new and modern homes, shops and factories, the effects of which began to be felt throughout Torbay. Whilst the traditional family summer holiday to Britain's resorts was under threat from cheaper holidays to sunnier climes, the resorts of South Devon responded by providing a wide range of facilities catering for short breaks, and entertainment for the young.

Gallows Gate stands on the hilltop overlooking Torquay and Torbay and adjacent to the ring road from Shiphay to Marldon. This historical site of Kingsdon, at the junction of three parishes, was the meeting place of a Saxon Hundred Court where cases would be tried, and also the site of the gallows where malefactors paid the penalty for crimes committed.

One of the foremost amateur theatre groups, formed in 1945, was the Torquay Operatic and Dramatic Society whose members performed plays at the Council-owned Babbacombe Theatre for more than 40 years. Around the 1960s, after purchasing an unused church at Meadfoot, a new title, TOADS Theatre Company was adopted. Built on their highly successful shows at the Meadfoot venue TOADS have become an enduring and popular attraction in Torquay entertainment. Now as the owners of the Little Theatre, Meadfoot, they can proudly claim to be the biggest amateur company in the South West of England with ten plays being produced each year.

Among their many acclaimed performances of TOADS 'The Ghost Train' and 'The Importance of Being Ernest' are shown here.

The women's section of the Paignton British Legion off to Blackpool for their Annual conference 1960.

In 1963, Torbay Disabled Fellowship launched an appeal for £1075 to provide a special coach and a garage at Rock Road. It was for the transport of ten disabled people, including room for two wheel-chairs. The prime mover was Mrs Arblaster seen on the left between the Chaplain and the patient, whose chair was lifted by an electrically operated ramp. Behind her is the new President of Fellowship Mr Phil Read Jnr who succeeded Miss D.B.Mottram on the right.

Members and organiser, Mrs E.Haggard, of the Torquay WRVS prepare to deliver hot meals to elderly people of the town.

Above: *Preparations for the 1963 yachting season and regatta as a fleet of 'E' class yachts take to the water at Beacon Quay slipway.*

Left: *A vast armada of sails assemble for the start of the 1962 class 'A' yachts in Torbay.*

Below: *The two photographs below record the memorable occasion in Torquay's yachting history when the yachting section of the 14th Olympiad was hosted by Torquay in August 1948. Twenty-two nations were represented with Argentina shown here after Greece. Here (below) the Canadian contingent march past bearing their national flag.*

Stirring things are happening at Torbay Hospital in the early 1960s with the staff and patients helping with the Christmas pudding

A civic reception was held for representatives of the South West Group of museums and art galleries meeting at Torre Abbey on 30 May 1963. The President, Mr H. Schubart, is shown centre front with the Mayor and Mayoress (Cllr & Mrs R.W. Kellow) and the Deputy Mayor and Mayoress (Cllr & Mrs W. Standley). On the right are the secretary of the Group, Mr G. Rye and Mrs R. Powell, President of the Torquay Natural History Society. Also representing the Torquay Museum & Natural History Society are Dr F. Wallis and Mr Beer. Behind the Mayoress is Mr A. Warhurst, Bristol City Museum who succeeded Dr Wallis as Director.

This striking bow fronted-building of modern flats was built on the site of Mr Edward Whitley's former home, Kilmorie. Erected around 1962, the flats overlook Meadfoot and the whole of Torbay, and were on sale at that time at £10 000. Opinion in Torbay was that the price was so prohibitive they would never sell. How wrong the pessimists were!

This early photograph contrasts the elegance of earlier buildings in Torbay with later buildings such as the flats (above). Hyde Dendy's Esplanade Hotel and Torbay cycle track in Paignton was built in 1883. Formerly two villas, Dendy joined them with a main entrance, surmounted with a tower and added the dormitory block on the left. The cycle track was laid out behind the hotel and used for national competitions. Later it became The Prince Regent and then The Inn on the Green.

Rosetor Hotel as seen in 1962. It was built by the Harvey brothers and leased to Baroness Burdett Coutts in 1862. She inherited from her father Sir Francis Burdett, powers of intellect that were stirred by the work of archaeologist William Pengelly. Immensely wealthy she was to assist financially in his exploration work.

This fifteenth century house shows it as restored by the Ministry of Works in 1962. It was built as a town house for the Kirkham family who originated at Blagdon Barton (two miles away) and whose name is given to a street in an old part of Paignton. A noted member of the family was Nicholas (1434-1516) after whom the Kirkham Chantry in the parish church is ascribed.

Torquay Harbour, Pavilion, Princess Theatre and Waldon Hill in the early 1960s. This comprehensive view of Torquay's seafront, and in the distance Chelston, records the development on top of Waldon as shown by the giant crane.

Things like this must come about if a town built in narrow valleys is to provide a car park convenient to shops and sufficient for a large summer population. This site is in Temperance Street between Union Street and Abbey Road, and photographed in 1964. This mammoth 40 tons rock-ripper is capable of moving 1000 tons of rock an hour.

Cuthbert Mayne was the first inter-denominational secondary school of its kind to be built in the County of Devon. It was officially blessed and opened on 11 June 1962, by the Roman Catholic Bishop of Plymouth, the Rt. Rev Mgr. Cyril Restieaux. It provided for 264 boys and girls within a catchment area of 16 miles.

The Old Police Station, Market Street, seen in 1965. It was built in 1876 for the local Board of Health and consists of 20 rooms, 2 halls and from back to front has a depth of 100 feet. When the new station in South Street was opened in 1944, the old premises were used as living quarters for police staff and later, firemen. The photographs show the frontage in Market Street (above), *the glass-roofed courtyard with cells on the left* (top right), *and the Courtroom.*

The Manor House in Middle Lincombe Road, Torquay, was begun by W.A. Goss in 1862 when Lord Haldon took up his residence there. Sir Francis Leyland Barratt bought it in 1906 and the figure of a lion bearing shield on the left of main front and the stone fluted garden vase nearby were brought by him from Venice. At the time this photograph was taken, in 1962, the house was a Rehabilitation Centre for the Blind.

Group Captain Leonard Cheshire VC, OM, DSO, DFC (above right), founded the first of his charity homes for the disabled not long after the end of the Second World War. Douglas House, one and half miles from Brixham, is set in a residential area with country and sea views and with provision for 23 nursing places and 6 residential places. The town is proud of the part it plays in sustaining this establishment which is regularly supported by local groups and associations. Here (above left) in 1962, in Victoria Park, Paignton, a volunteer is broadcasting an appeal for a 'mile of pennies' through the town.

Torquay Pavilion in the mid 1960s.

Torquay's famous Pavilion was a citadel of entertainment for many years. This George IV style building had, during its forty years of classical concerts, military bands, plays and concert parties provided a variety of social entertainment which attracted audiences from all parts of Devon. For many years the Pavilion orchestra, under the direction of its founder Ernest Goss, was host to many famous performers including Paul Robeson, Dame Nellie Melba and John McCormack. At Festival Concerts, guest conductors were Sir Edward Elgar, Sir Henry Wood, Sir Malcolm Sergeant, Sir Adrian Boult and many others.

Financial problems however, resulting partly from apathy, saw the orchestra give its final concert in 1953. Although demolition was considered by the council, the Pavilion was saved by a group called 'Friends of the Pavilion' and is now a listed building. Ernest W.Goss, whose musical services to the town covered a period of 50 years, died in 1964, aged 81.

The demise of the Torquay Municipal Orchestra in 1953 came as a bitter blow to the town. From its formal opening in 1912 the orchestra maintained its standard of entertainment for forty-one years until its final concert in April 1953. Among the members of the Torquay Municipal Orchestra who served under the direction of Ernest Goss were: R. Darrock (Deputy Conductor), R.E. Foster (Leader), W. Burrans, H. Littlepage, T.G. Clubb, J. Hudson, P. Abbot, W. Foster, R. Dunning, J. Hawkins, E. Smith, J. Thomson, A.Fiske, J. Clinch, R. Secluna, E. Cook, E. Gillard, R. Lamming, P. Stevens, P. Quilter, G. Ellis, H. Southwood, P. Coles and S. Copeland. Among the ladies were Mrs Quilter, Miss Hartley, Miss Hatch, and Miss Whales.

Mayor Choosing in Torquay, 1965. The retiring Mayor, Alderman R.P. Williams is seen congratulating his successor Alderman A.E. Elson. In the lower picture is seen the Mayor's procession to St Matthew's church, Chelston. Alderman Elson and acting Town Clerk, Mr L. Womersley are followed by the Deputy Mayor, Alderman R.W. Kellow and Ex-Mayor, Alderman R.P. Williams. The Mace Bearer is John Smith.

The heart of Torquay, May 1965, when frantic efforts were being made to complete the traffic changes before the onset of the summer season. Opposite the Old Town Hall in Union Street premises have been demolished and the site prepared for the roundabout. On the right down traffic uses Union Street, and two-way traffic is still using Abbey Road on the left. The foremost bus is trying to negotiate its way up to Pimlico. This scene is in sharp contrast with the picture showing the area in 1907 (left) with an electric tram passing the Town Hall and pedestrians walking in the road.

A splendid view of the beach taken from Rock Walk on a fine sunny day, early summer, 1961.

Members of the Torbay branch of WRNS on the way to the Parish Church Service in St Marychurch, 26 May 1963. Carrying the standard is Mrs J. Dobson.

A contingent from Torquay's adopted warship, the Frigate HMS Torquay march through Union Street to the Town Hall on 25 February 1961, where they were entertained by the Mayor Alderman J.F. Haarer. Unfortunately, as can be seen from the pohotgraph, the visit was marred by heavy rain.

A night view of the Princess Theatre fully illuminated 1961.

Paignton Festival Hall, built on the sea front in the 1960s, became a mecca of outstanding entertainment for thousands of visitors and residents alike, and was host to a multitude of stage and television stars during the 32 years of its lifetime. This first picture shows the early stages of construction and the second, the finished building pending the arrival of the supreme Black and White Minstrel Show (above right). In 1999 the Festival hall was demolished to make way for the Apollo Cinema which now replaces it.

This beautiful photograph shows folk dancing in the historic grounds of Oldway in June 1964.

This is the Brixham Ladies Choir as they were in the late 1960s early 1970s. Now known as 'The Riviera Singers', their concerts for charities reach far and wide. Among those pictured are: Stella Manning, Margaret Waters, Yvonne King, Anne Adams, Iris Davis, Betty Foster, Leonora Douglas, Marjorie Douglas, Irene Green, Iris Pullen, Airlys Clarke, Barbara King, Alice Bagg, Mary Dyer, and Diane Harding.

Palk Arch, Torquay, 1961. The Arch, built in 1832, was by 1903 the subject of much contention for in that year it looked so shabby that the manager of the adjoining bank wanted to demolish it and soon proceeded to do so. At once the Haldon Estate claimed its possession and ordered the Bank to restore it. All that was needed was a coat of paint which was given by Whiteway & Ball Co. who used it as a direction post to their office. By 1916 the Electric Theatre Co. owned it, using it for advertising as shown on the facing pillars. The arch was finally demolished in February 1962.

In February, 1962, the Arch that had spanned Palk Street for 130 years and had stood as a memorial to General Lawrence by the Palk family was demolished to make way for the provision of coach stands which the Town Council were hoping to set up in Palk Street to replace existing road-side stands. Provision for buses on the busy route 12 was made at Marine Square. During the summer of 1959 'Atlanteans' first made their appearance on this route.

Oldway in the late 1960s and (inset) as it was in the 1920s.

Summertime visitors relaxing in the gardens at Oldway c.1965. In the background is the Rotunda, built as a pavilion for horses and containing a marble-tiled pool.

Part of the magnificent ceiling at Oldway, inspiration of the wealthy Paris Singer.

Although Isaac Singer, the sewing machine millionaire, was the great benefactor who built Paignton's famous Oldway Mansion, it was his third son Paris who spent another fortune in remodelling it in the style of the Palace of Versailles. The interior is dominated by a vast and beautiful multi-coloured marble staircase above which is the magnificent painted ceiling.

Before the County Borough was formed in 1967 it became a regular custom for Paignton Councillors, employees and their wives to meet at Oldway for their annual dinner. Here, among those gathered on the historic elegant staircase in 1949, are Mr and Mrs Sam Hodgson, Mr and Mrs Les Hicks, Mr and Mrs Spanton, Mr and Mrs Shilston Sharp, Mr and Mrs George Stabb, Major and Mrs Bengley, Mr and Mrs Craze, Mrs Flemons, Messrs Battershill, Thick, Sercombe, Peters and Matthews.

Standing on the steps at Oldway are the last members of Paignton Urban District Council before its disbandment in 1967. Front row (left to right): G.K. Foster, Mrs Fraser-James, Jimmy Tremeer, Frank Martin, Ken Walker, Jack Kingsland, Wally Beasley, Mrs Heath, Mrs Walton, Mrs Basildon, John Cole. Middle row: John Hayman, Bill Preston, Syd Elliott, Quenton Buckland, John Ellswood, Bill Chidgey, Leon Jones, Jack Bennett. Back row: Fred Bidgood, Ray Snell, Frank Charlesworth, Arthur Agar, John Bewley, Graham Lorraine.

A Christmas party at Rosehill in 1966. The new room (right) was provided by the Hospital Management Committee with the county Council sharing the cost.

Originally this building was the Salem Chapel, built by Robert Stark, minister until his death in 1854. It was then converted into the School of Science under the name of the Vivian Institute and in 1918 became the School of Arts and Crafts. Situated in Braddons Hill Road West, in 1966 it became the Torquay branch of the South Devon Technical College School of Art, the other two being at Paignton and Newton Abbot.

This excellent photograph of Castle Circus was taken in 1967 from a crane 90 feet above the triangle, a decade after the demolition of the site previously known as Brock's Corner which had remained empty, surrounded by a corrugated iron fence. Union Street in the foreground passes the Electricity Showrooms and continues on to Fleet Street. In Castle Circus, the Town Hall faces the Regal cinema. In the distance is Stentiford Hill which is approached from Castle Circus by Castle Road, where on the left is the Castle YMCA Club.

Brock's Corner at the junction of Union Street and Tor Hill Road in 1900, when Tor Hill House on the left was Brock's Furniture Shop. It was demolished in the 1950s and in 1967 additional offices for the new County Borough were erected with shops on the ground floor. On the right side of the road, White's Exchange Mart was later replaced by the Electricity showrooms. The photographed occasion was the procession of the Town Council to Upton Church.

In this 1966 photo, Brock's furniture store has been removed. Union Street and the Town Hall are on the right, Tor Hill Road on left, joined by Higher Union Lane on near side of Masonic Hall (extreme left). Hopes for a noble building to replace Brock's Corner gave way to a plan for shops and offices.

Here, in 1961, on the grassy bank above Cockington Court is a host of golden daffodils that compelled the photographer to record the scene.

Churston Ferrers Court and Church in the mid 1960s. The name Ferrers is derived from the thirteenth century family of Sir Hugh Ferrers, with the village being a ward of Brixham. The village is proud of its enchanting Churston Court Inn, of Saxon Manor vintage, for here lived the Saxon Earl, Ulf, and his son Judhael as Lords of Totnes. Its importance is evidenced by the pictorial representation on the Mayor of Torbay's chain of office.

In 1962, the replica of Sir Francis Drake's ship Golden Hind *was secured alongside Haldon Pier for a time as a showpiece for visitors. The ship was built for the Westward Television series on the life of Drake, and was later sold.*

The start of the men's long-distance swim from Beacon Cove, Torquay, to Brixham and back in 1960 – a distance of approximately four miles each way. The long board by the rocks was used as a diving board for many years but in time rusted away.

Paignton's crowded beach at the peak of the summer in 1964. Such was its popularity as a family resort that it was not unusual for the local population to almost double in size. This four-man crew are finding some difficulty in steering their racing skiff through the vast crowd.

This was Torquay's ten-pin bowling alley in Union Street, above Castle Circus in the 1960s. It was built for the Excel Bowling Co to the design of well-known builder Mr E. Narracott at a cost of about £250 000. The building itself was interesting as it appeared as a one storey structure in Higher Union Street but as three storeys in Upton Valley. With 18 bowling lanes it was called the Galaxy Bowling Club in those days. Sold in 1990 it became Rileys Snooker club.

What a difference a season makes. The top picture shows Beacon Cove in the late Autumn of 1963 and in the second, the same beach in the following August with capacity crowds. At the water's edge bathers are sitting on the outlet pipe from the swimming bath. On the high ground above the beach is the Princes Hotel and on the extreme right a glimpse of a part of the Imperial Hotel.

An impressive view of the 55 000 ton Aircraft Carrier HMS Eagle *with ships line astern overtaking the Royal Yacht* Britannia *about ten miles from Torquay on 29 July 1969. HMS* Eagle *at this time carried ninety aircraft.*

The departure of the Royal Family on the Royal Barge from Haldon Pier, Torquay on 28 July 1969. With Her Majesty is Lord Roborough, Lord Lieutenant of Devon, followed by the Duke of Edinburgh in the uniform of the Admiral of the Fleet. Behind their father are Prince Charles and Princess Anne.

HMY Britannia *at anchor in Torbay on 28 July 1969, to the East of the assembled fleet of warships which fired a salute when the barge with the Royal Party arrived on Britannia. The yacht is flying the Royal Standard at the mainmast; that of the Lord High Admiral at the foremast and the Union Jack at the mizzen. Below this can be seen the veranda deck from which the Queen waved to the warships in the great steam-past.*

Here the Queen is presenting new Colours in the upper hangar instead of the flight deck because of high winds in Torbay. On the rostrum HM the Queen can be seen with the rest of the royal family. The flag is being dipped in salute by Lieutenant N.S. Seddon-Brown while the crew stand to attention.

Following the presentation of new Colours by the Queen, a fly-past of some 90 Fleet Air Arm planes took place watched by the Royal Family from the flight deck. Later this was followed by a steam-past of many of the assembled ships which the Queen viewed from HMY Britannia. July 1969.

This must be one of the last photographs of Paignton's beloved Deller's Café, taken just before it was demolished in 1965 after well over fifty years as a meeting place for the town's residents and holiday visitors. It also served as a focus for winter dinners, dances and parties as it could accommodate up to a thousand people at any one time.

Fleet Street as we once knew it, c.1920. The facing large building in Fleet Street is at the junction of the road leading to The Terrace. Now a listed building it was for some years the Devon & Exeter Savings Bank, with above it, the offices of Almy & Thomas, solicitors.

Two way traffic in Fleet Street in the mid 1960s showing shops familiar to Torquinians. On the left is the department store of J.F. Rockhey and on the right beyond the tall lamp-standard the General Post Office. In the foreground, on the left of the stationary van, are steps, then leading down to Swan Street and George Street.

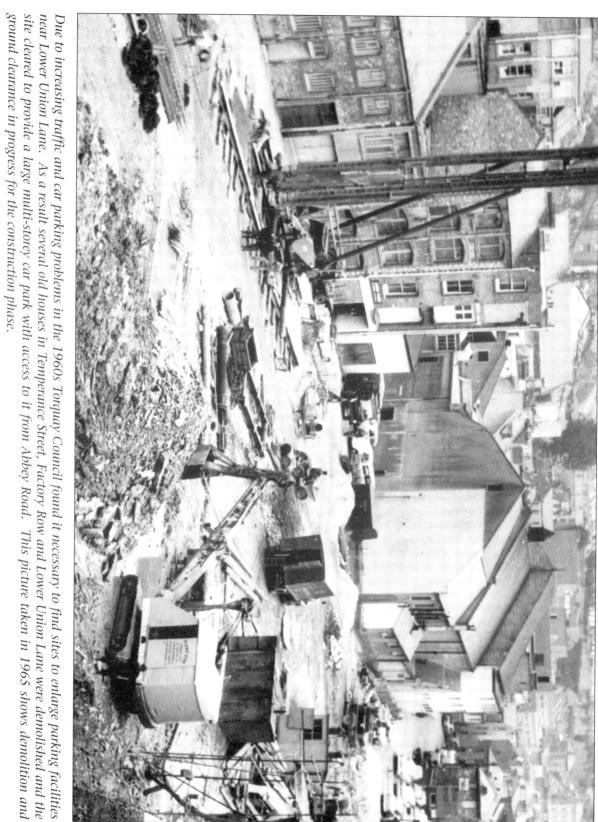

Due to increasing traffic and car parking problems in the 1960s Torquay Council found it necessary to find sites to enlarge parking facilities near Lower Union Lane. As a result several old houses in Temperance Street, Factory Row and Lower Union Lane were demolished and the site cleared to provide a large multi-storey car park with access to it from Abbey Road. This picture taken in 1965 shows demolition and ground clearance in progress for the construction phase.

9 – 'History is Now'

While the following photographs may fall outside the era of the 1950s and 1960s, the decades of 'Torbay's Golden Years', they provide a vital record of the disorder that ensued during the Fleet Walk development in the years 1987-1989 and serve as a reminder of 'how it used to be'. The changes from the old to the new were sweeping, and not to everyone's satisfaction. Old buildings have gone, familiar old business premises have vanished and with them much of Torquay's endearing history. But while we may look back with affection to the bygones of yesteryear, new generations will remind us that 'history is now'.

This photograph shows the early stages of construction and the signs of things to come in the late 1980s. On the left by the railings is the slip road of Braddon's Hill Road West where the Torquay Times newspaper had their offices for many years. Note the relatively rudimentary barriers alongside the road and the lack of protection between pedestrians, traffic and the construction site. A far cry from today's health and safety conscious practices.

A later stage showing the growing state of chaos in Fleet Street, around 1988. Traffic and pedestrians are competing for space while demolition proceeds apace.

Not the aftermath of enemy bombing in World War II but the latter stages of demolition before the build-ing and construction of the new Fleet Walk. On the left in the deep shadows the road runs up to The Terrace and St John's Church. The debris from the demolition extended over a very large area and created many complex traffic diversions.

The middle stage of the Fleet Walk project. The massive accumulation of debris has been removed and the site prepared for the start of reconstruction. Centre, is the Devon & Exeter Savings Bank building and further right, the Strand begins. The shadowy space on the left below the crane and between the two large white buildings, is all that is left of busy Swan Street, at the corner of which stood Slade's, the general grocers' warehouse. The area of apparent desolation was formerly Abbey Place, George Street, Swan Street, Marine Square, etc.

Here, in the early stages of completion, an intricate mass of steel girders tower above the ever struggling Fleet Street traffic in 1988-89.

Nearing completion Fleet Walk (originally called the Winter Garden) building is topped by a handsome ornamental dome of copper. Entry to the vast middle story car park within would be by turning off the road and driving into the large dark space on the left.

10 – Torquay Museum

The majority of photographs included in this book are drawn from Torquay Museum's archives, many of which have been donated by local newspapers, professional photographers and individuals.

The museum was founded in 1844 by Torquay Natural History Society and is Devon's oldest museum. It houses the foremost collection of Kent's Cavern artefacts, and papers from the famous archaeological excavation by William Pengelly. Recently the museum has undergone a major refurbishment thanks to a Heritage Lottery Fund grant and is an essential attraction for all visitors to South Devon. Physical access around the museum has been transformed for visitors with mobility problems and pushchairs. The work has also ensured the preservation of the beautiful Victorian building.

In 2001 the museum unveiled the new Devon Farmhouse gallery, café and gift shop. The new TimeArk Gallery will house the natural science collections showing the evolution of the environment and habitat of the local area using hands-on interpretative displays. Agatha Christie fans can use their own investigating skills on the updated displays relating to the world famous crime writer, who was born in Torquay.

Designed by William Harvey, the original Museum building is an excellent example of Venetian-Gothic architecture. Just inside the entrance of the large and imposing foyer, a sixteenth century Spanish sea-chest is displayed, reputedly from an Armada galleon, and a reminder of Torquay's association with the battle against the Spanish fleet. The photograph on the left shows the refurbished hallway.

Among the Museums facilities is a library of over 10 000 books, and galleries displaying local history, the flora and fauna of the region, geology and social history. There is also an impressive permanent exhibition devoted to the life and work of Agatha Christie, many of whose works were written from her home in Torquay. Below is shown one of the original galleries.

The important 'Old Devon Farmhouse' Gallery is based upon the collection of Charles Hay Laycock who lived in the South Devon area in the early years of the twentieth century. Aware of the changes in the countryside around him he began to collect everyday articles and utensils, dating from the sixteenth to the late nineteenth centuries, from farms and cottages, particularly on and around Dartmoor. This now survives as the nation's largest collection of domestic furnishings, tools, ornaments and utensils devoted to a single county, and is of major importance to those studying the domestic life in rural communities.

*The hub of Torquay as it was in the 1960s. The photograph, taken in
1962, shows the Old Town Hall at the junction with Union Street
(on the right), Abbey Road (on the left), and Fleet Street in the foreground.
At this time Abbey Road still had two-way traffic.*

OTHER TITLES OF LOCAL INTEREST FROM HALSGROVE

HALSGROVE BOOKS BY FRANK PEARCE

The Book of Torbay - Frank Pearce

The Book of Paignton - Frank Pearce

The Book of Dawlish - Frank Pearce

OTHER HALSGROVE TITLES OF LOCAL INTEREST

A History of the Torbay Lifeboats - Alan Salsbury

The Ellacombe Book - Sydney Langmead

Devon in the Great War 1914-1918 - Gerald Wasley

Devon At War 1939-1945 - Gerald Wasley

Devon in the 1930s - Gerald Wasley

Devon Firefighter - Iain Rice

Devon at the Cinema - Gordon Chapman

SELECTED DARTMOOR TITLES FROM HALSGROVE

Dartmoor Stone - Stephen Woods

Dartmoor Stone Crosses - W. Harrison

Dartmoor Boundary Stones - Dave Brewer

Dartmoor Century I - Simon Butler

Dartmoor Century II - Simon Butler

Dartmoor Prison - An Illustrated History Vol 1 - Ron Joy

Dartmoor Prison - An Illustrated History Vol 2 - Ron Joy

Dartmoor Artists - Brian Le Messurier